TALKING TO TEENS

ABOUT

DATING AND SEX

A Christian Approach
to
Relationships, Dating and Sexual Purity

by

Scott ♥ *Cheri Scheer*

Published by Family Ministries
Printed in the United States of America
by Faith Printing
Cover by Jeff Martin

ISBN 1-931600-09-0

www.familyministries.net

TABLE OF CONTENTS

Introduction 5

Chapter 1   Forming a Value System 11

Chapter 2   The Great Counterfeit 18

Chapter 3   Familiarity 24

Chapter 4   How Bonding Takes Place 39

Chapter 5   Godly Guidelines 48

Chapter 6   The Covenant of Marriage 59

Chapter 7   Making the Choice 68

INTRODUCTION

We were teenagers in the sixties. Among other things, that era was noted for its devastating effect on moral standards. It is irrelevant to debate whether it was the influence of rock and roll or a war that no one wanted to fight that caused the change. Many have concluded that it was because prayer and Bible reading were removed from our public schools–because the traditional value system that formed our society disintegrated. Being a Christian teen in the sexual revolution posed a tremendous challenge. There was a constant tug of war between adhering to values of our parents and keeping pace with an ever changing society.

Early in our marriage we were involved with youth ministry. We understood the potential pitfalls that accompany not following God's plan and purpose for relationships, dating and sexual purity. We were married in the early seventies when social scientists predicted that fifty percent of all marriages would end in divorce–a new milestone for our culture! We were aware that the philosophy of sexual permissiveness contributed to this frightening phenomena.

The teens under our ministry received a buffet of teaching on God's plan for relationships and preparation for marriage. It didn't take long for us to realize how important it is for the parents to understand the material which was being presented to their teenagers.

We hear parents continually complaining about the outside influences on their children. They criticize the schools, television, movies, books, and even youth pastors. It's the old blame game. Everyone else is at fault. Studies have shown that by far the number one influence in a teen's life is his parent(s). Today's teens are more apt to steal, cheat, drink, do drugs, have sex out of marriage, participate in criminal activity or commit suicide than any other generation. Only four percent have a personal relationship with Jesus Christ.

In spite of all of this bad news, God has a call upon this generation. He has called this generation to stand up for righteousness, to reverse the tide of sin and restore the family.

A note to teens: We respect you for reading this book and taking time to explore what God has to say about relationships and sex. After you read this, give it to your parents and ask them read it. Better yet, read it to them and discuss it with them. The decisions you make concerning relationships, dating and sexual purity will dramatically affect your future. This book is designed to give you practical information and godly counsel. Once you've heard it, what you do with it is up to you.

A note to parents: Blessed is the parent who reads this book and instills these principles within his teenager(s)! Malachi 4:6 tells us that there is a day of restoration coming to the family. It says, *"The hearts of the fathers will be turned to the children."* As a parent, **your** heart needs to turn to your children first. Don't preach at them, don't manipulate or control them. Set an example and show them the value in following God's plan.

We have served in the full-time ministry for more than thirty years. During that time we also managed to raise three children–Rochelle, Kimberly, and James. Raising our own children, and especially counseling other parents who were raising teenagers, challenged us to author *The Bonding Process* (a simple guide for teens to understand dating and sex from a biblical perspective) and *Talking to Teens About Dating and Sex*. We have noted that there are certain foundational principles which need to be solidly implemented in order to successfully guide teenagers through this challenging period of their lives.

Throughout life, bonding takes place on spiritual, emotional, and physical levels. The bonds which are formed can be healthy, building the individual's spirit-man and self-esteem, or detrimental, with far-reaching negative effects. The understanding of and application of scriptural principles combined with a willingness to follow the guidance of the Holy Spirit determines the bonding that takes place and its effects upon the individual.

This book will acquaint the reader with God's design for bonding, His principles for establishing godly relationships and standards for sexual purity. It has been designed to assist parents in providing direction for their own children, and to equip those in full-time ministry to instruct those entrusted to their care in biblical standards. It also has been fashioned as a guide for teenagers and young adults, to help them understand how relationships are formed and how to establish guidelines that will insure sexual purity.

The stories shared in this book come out of years of experience. The names have been changed, but the circumstances are not restricted to locality or time. Stories like these happen every day. Often they happen to good Christian young people from nice homes. After you have read these stories, we would encourage you to think about what you would have done if you were in the same situation.

From our hearts to your home,
Scott ♥ Cheri

John was fifteen and interested in a nice girl in his church named Dianne. John's parents set high standards for their children and wouldn't let him date until he was sixteen. His problem was that his birthday was a month away, but he wanted to take Dianne to a dance the next weekend. He shared his dilemma with a seventeen year old buddy named Bob, who attended the same church that John did. Bob suggested that John's parents might let him take Dianne to the dance if it was a double-date. John talked to his Dad. Surprisingly, his dad agreed, reasoning that as long as John and Dianne were with another couple (especially with a boy from their own church) things would be under control. John's excitement grew as the big night approached. Bob had his own car, so the four of them went to the dance in style. About an hour into the dance Bob grabbed John and said, "Let's leave. Maybe we'll get lucky and get a little." John laughed, but felt uncomfortable when he told Dianne that they were leaving. Bob drove out of town and pulled into a wooded area off the road. He told John and Dianne to get in the front seat. As they did, Bob and his girlfriend got into the back. It wasn't long before both John and Dianne became embarrassed by the behavior in the back seat! At first they talked more loudly in an effort to cover up the noises. At one point an article of intimate apparel landed on John's head. Bob laughed, calling out, "What base are you on? All I hear is talking up there. You two need to get with it!" At that point John and Dianne got out of the car and walked back to town.

Chapter 1

FORMING A VALUE SYSTEM

As the Sunday School class quieted down, the youth pastor opened with prayer. He proceeded to ask if anyone had any questions before he began the lesson. He had always encouraged the students to be open in sharing their thoughts, and this had paved the way for some valuable discussions. Today was to be no exception. A young woman raised her hand and asked, "Does God really say it's wrong to have sex before marriage, or is that something parents and pastors say just to scare us?"

Surprising as it may seem, this is a question commonly asked by young people. Many teens do not have a clear understanding of biblically-based standards for sexual abstinence and purity. They have developed a system of values by which they relate to the opposite sex. That value system is often formulated either without a clear understanding of God's Word or without a relationship of accountability to God.

The primary cause for this is the parents' lack of understanding of the biblical principles. A parent's lack of relationship with his child and inability to communicate with him also contributes. Adding to this is confusion caused by the influence of peers and secular information provided within the school system, on television, in periodicals, or by social agencies.

Most parents address the dating issue by setting an age at which their kids can date, but never discussing how relationships are formed. They address the sex issue by explaining how people have babies and warning their kids not to have sex. Many parents also add, " . . . and you better not come home pregnant!" Some give a little added input as they explain that sex causes AIDS and sexually transmitted diseases. And they may advise, " . . . so if you're going to have sex, make sure you use protection!"

Very few parents take the time to properly address these issues and explain biblical principles to their kids. Not many parents help their kids grow in relationship with God through the years so that by the time they are teenagers they have an understanding of their accountability to Him. They mistakenly assume the church will address the issue of sexual standards through the ministry of the youth group and the youth pastor.

Unfortunately, too few churches take a strong stand against premarital sex and sexual impurity. Our society has consistently lowered its standards in this area, which has adversely affected the churches' standards and the value systems of Christian families. A survey of 1,400 evangelical Christian teens found that more than 36 percent said they did not think premarital sex was morally wrong. In a society that defends the rights of the homosexual and allows minors to obtain contraceptives and abortions without parental knowledge or consent, the church should be the voice that expounds the truth! Church leadership has the responsibility to instruct parents and teenagers in biblical standards, accountability and relationship to God as it pertains to value systems, morality and relationships.

Our culture teaches *safe sex* as an attempt to deter unwanted births and disease. God's standard is *no sex* outside of marriage.

It is important for both parents and teens to understand God's plan for human sexuality and the bonding process. Fulfillment in one's marriage and sexuality are achieved only when God's principles are followed.

Society is continually becoming more confused about sexual standards. In spite of increased education, scientific discovery and the information highway, there is an increase in people making self-destructive choices. There *is* a lot of information available, but much of it is wrong! Television has sold us a distorted view of what relationships are all about.

We are in a battle against demonic powers which want to destroy the family unit and the holiness of the marriage covenant. That age-old nemesis, the sinful nature, is bent on wreaking havoc with God's wonderful plan. Values and standards have been watered-down. In a desire to be accepted by their peers, Christian teens, who have committed themselves to virginity, have succumbed to the pressure to lower their standards in regard to sexual activity, becoming involved in everything but the sex act itself.

Many of our heroes and television stars are corrupt. The moral attitudes displayed by our governmental leadership are not what they used to be. In years gone by integrity, character and a strong value system were priorities when electing government officials and employing teachers, coaches and care givers. A recent survey revealed that the majority of the population feels that the morality of governmental officials should be kept private–it should not matter as long it does not directly interfere with job performance.

Making the right choices can be a difficult process, unless you are guided by a value system based on a strong foundation of truth from the Word of God. The Bible gives direction as to where you should get direction. Psalm 1:1-3 says, *"Blessed is the man who walks not in the counsel of the ungodly, nor stands in the path of sinners, nor sits in the seat of the scornful; but his delight is in the law of the Lord, and in His law he meditates day and night."*

Listening to peers, sports heroes or television idols for advice is not an option for the child of God. God's people need to find the truth about life-producing concepts which will bring them health and success. John 5:39 shows where to find them.

"You search the Scriptures, for in them you think you have eternal life; and these are they which testify of Me."

Jesus is our example of the truth. John 14:6 says, *"I am the way, the truth, and the life. No one comes to the Father except through Me."*

Adults and teenagers alike need to understand that there is always a consequence for every action. Every choice begins the momentum to change the rest of your life. Galatians 6:7-9 states, *"Do not be deceived.*

God is not mocked; for whatever a man sows, that he will also reap. For he who sows to his flesh will of the flesh reap corruption, but he who sows to the Spirit will of the Spirit reap everlasting life."

Heather was fourteen and had never dated–but she certainly was interested in boys. One day her mother announced to her that she and Heather's Dad were going out with some friends who were visiting from out of town. Their eighteen year old son, Jim, was with them, and he was going to take her to a movie. The parents thought it would be fun for their children to get together and have fun, too.

Although Heather was very mature looking for her age, she was very naive. Her mother had never talked with her about dating, sex or setting guidelines for behavior with the opposite sex. She did tell Heather that Jim was a nice boy from a good family and that going out with him was a real privilege. She said that this family was quite influential and had a good standing in the country club. She told Heather to make sure that Jim had a good time!

Jim showed up in a fancy red sports car. Heather was impressed with how handsome he was. Needless to say she was feeling quite grown up. They went to a movie and Jim escorted her to a seat in the back row.

When the movie started, Jim started massaging Heather's hand. He then put his arm around her and began to fondle her. Jim started kissing her and gently rubbing her legs. Heather was a little nervous, but from what she had heard from friends and had seen at movies and on TV, she thought this was normal dating behavior. After the movie, Jim took her to a beach where he removed Heather's clothing and introduced her to sex.

Chapter 2

THE GREAT COUNTERFEIT

"And the Lord God caused a deep sleep to fall on Adam, and he slept; and he took one of his ribs, and closed up the flesh in its place. The rib which the Lord God had taken from man He made into a woman, and He brought her to the man. And God saw everything that he had made and, behold, it was very good." Genesis 2:22, 1:31

God had a perfect plan. Part of that wonderful plan included the creation of a man and a woman. They were beautiful to behold, made in the image of God. God placed within them the ability to love, help and care for one another. They had perfect communication–emotionally, physically, and spiritually. They were totally committed to meeting one another's needs. Adam could sense Eve's needs and desires and would quickly respond to her without being asked. They had no insecurities, fears or frustrations. They had total trust in each other.

Spiritually they lived in perfect harmony with God. Devoid of guilt and shame, they rejoiced in their relationship. They sensed His presence at every moment and walked in perfect communion with Him. He placed within this perfect creation an intricate system of nerves, organs, glands and a brain that could record and decipher each sensation. God gave the man and the woman a desire to touch and be touched. The sense of touch would provide many pleasurable emotions. The ecstasy found within the sense of touch would become even more heightened as Adam engaged in sexual intercourse with his precious Eve.

When a climax was reached in the sexual act, Adam and Eve would attain the highest level of security, love and oneness that could be experienced in the physical. It would be second only to the oneness they had in the spiritual with God. Having bonded emotionally and physically, Adam and Eve together would contemplate the words which Adam had spoken.

"This is now bone of my bones, and flesh of my flesh; she shall be called woman, because she was taken out of man. Therefore shall a man leave his father and his mother, and shall cleave unto his wife; and they shall be one flesh." Genesis 2:23

God created sex and sexual desire. Within the confines of God's plan, sexual intercourse is one of life's paramount experiences. By God's design, it was the highest expression of Adam and Eve's love, the culmination of a deep friendship, the realization of a relationship blessed by God, the ultimate reflection of a total commitment to one another. It sounds wonderful, doesn't it? That's what God planned in the beginning–and still wants for His creation today!

"And they heard the sound of the Lord God walking in the garden in the cool of the day, and Adam and his wife hid themselves from the presence of the Lord God among the trees of the garden. Then the Lord God called to Adam and said to him, Where are you? So he said, I heard Your voice in the garden, and I was afraid because I was naked; and I hid myself. And He said, Who told you that you were naked? Have you eaten from the tree of which I commanded you that you should not eat?" Genesis 3:8

What had happened? Why did Adam and Eve suddenly feel inhibited in God's presence? They had sinned, and that sin had destroyed the encasement of perfection. The harmony, innocence and holiness were gone. Their sudden concern about their nakedness was an outward manifestation of a deeper spiritual problem. Their spiritual oneness with God was corrupted. Wanting to hide their physical nakedness was a poor attempt at covering their spiritual stigma. Their sin had found them out. It wasn't their physical nakedness that was the problem–it was the condition of their hearts that they really didn't want God to see.

Sin had caused a breach in God's perfect plan for man. The relationship between God and man would not be the same. The relationship between Adam and Eve would not be the same either. Their lives would be wrought with hardship. They no longer would walk in the purity, innocence and fulfillment that God intended for them.

As time ensued, the devil would continue to distort relationships. Throughout time he would continue his effort to destroy the most sacred of human experiences–sexual intimacy between the man and woman. This sexual communion, intended by God to enhance and produce life, would be twisted, perverted and counterfeited by the devil to produce destruction and death for man.

The devil assaults the sexual area because the physical communion of the covenant marriage relationship so closely corresponds to the covenant relationship God has with his highest creation, mankind. The counterfeits he produces are sexual involvement without commitment, cohabitation without accountability, love without devotion and marriage without covenant. For the millions of children who have been sexually abused, for the women who have been raped or misused, for those trapped by prostitution, sodomy, bestiality, pornography and adultery, intimacy has lost the beauty that God designed.

Jerry had dated a little through high school but never had been serious with anyone. He often wondered if he would ever find a girl that he would love enough to marry. While attending college he met Laura. He knew from the start that there was a future for this relationship. They immediately fell in love and he was convinced that Laura was his future wife. They were compatible in every way. Every outing was an adventure full of laughter and love.

Jerry and Laura had a deep faith in God and often talked about guidelines for their sexual conduct. Their growing love made it more and more difficult to keep their hands off each other.

One night, as they were discussing the issue, Laura started to cry. Trembling through the tears, she shared with Jerry that after her senior prom she went to a party where she had some champagne and her boyfriend took advantage of the situation and had sex with her. Jerry felt sick in the pit of his stomach. On the one hand he wanted to comfort her for he knew it took a lot for her to share this with him, but on the other hand an anger rose up in him.

The relationship was definitely strained for the next few weeks. Jerry was a virgin and had always believed that he would remain so until he got married. He became very bitter and found it difficult to forgive her. The two planned a weekend camp out thinking that time away together might bring the healing. During that weekend they started having sexual relations with each other. Jerry reasoned that perhaps their intimacy would put the relationship back on track. Within weeks they broke up, hurt and confused.

Chapter 3

FAMILIARITY

Forming relationships happens as you become familiar with others. The relationship deepens as you spend time together. As you become familiar with others, a bond is formed. An old saying goes, *"Familiarity breeds contempt."* The basis for this saying lies in judgements. As we get to know more about a person, we discover their value system, idiosyncracies and habits, and we make judgement calls. Based on our own ideals and ideas, we either like or dislike the individual.

The term *familiarity* refers to acquaintance, intimacy, liberty, awareness, casualness, closeness, disrespect, ease, experience, friendship, impropriety, intrusiveness, knowledge, license and understanding. The dictionary defines familiarity as *"Free and intimate behavior, actions of formality, close acquaintance."* Familiarity can be positive or negative and occurs on three levels–the spiritual, physical, and emotional.

You become spiritually familiar with others as you pray, worship or share a spiritual experience with them. You may feel a spiritual familiarity with a pastor, Sunday school teacher, prayer partner or the person who led you to the Lord. As you develop spiritual awareness of others, ascertaining their relationship with God, appreciating their style of worship and focusing on their needs in prayer, you become bonded in the spiritual sense. One purpose the church fulfills is that of developing a oneness in the Spirit for those of like faith.

We may become emotionally familiar with many individuals, including our parents, siblings, grandparents, aunts and uncles, mentors and friends. Emotional familiarity takes place when you share your thoughts, feelings, dreams, desires, hopes and fears. The more you share, the more you bond. Just sharing your opinion with someone can produce a bond–although it sometimes is a negative bond. If you disagree with someone, you may wish to avoid them to keep from an unpleasant confrontation.

You become familiar physically with another person by sharing your physical self with them, either visually or through touch. Physical familiarity progresses by degrees, depending upon the amount of physical involvement. For example, when a young man and woman are attracted to each other at a church meeting, they have favorably noticed each other's appearance. The physical bond established is visual. If they meet while wearing swim suits at the beach, the visual bond could be stronger. With more revelation comes a greater bond. When two people meet and shake hands, there is a physical bond, although it is very slight. If a teenage boy and girl go out together and hold hands, the physical bond that forms is a little deeper than just shaking hands. The amount of touching deepens the bond.

God has a plan and purpose for us in the area of bonding and becoming familiar with the opposite sex. Depending on how it is directed, familiarity can either strengthen or destroy a relationship.

In the fifties, we witnessed a major transition in the morality of our country. A new permissiveness invaded the American culture. The introduction of rock 'n roll, the accessibility and increase of publications, and the expansion of the television and movie industries amplified this new freedom. By way of the screen, one could now enter another couple's bedroom and observe their intimacy. The sexual revolution of the sixties professed the benefits of *free love*. However, love was not, is not and never will be free. There is always a cost associated with love. Unless physical familiarity is handled with care, it can prompt promiscuity, which opens a Pandora's box of physical, psychological and spiritual maladies.

The so-called *liberated* ones, with their profession of open marriages, legalized prostitution, nude beaches and uncensored media, have not only encouraged premarital sex, but also have left a wake of statistics that would shame Sodom and Gomorrah. The age-old theorem, *the more we know, the more we want to know; the more we see, the more we want to see; the more we have, the more we want to have,* has validity.

Education and knowledge are not the enemies of godliness. Hosea 4:6 tells us, *"My people perish due to the lack of knowledge."*

What God's people need to question is: What is being taught, who is doing the teaching and what methods are being used to instruct? Biblical principles need to be taught. Those who hold the Word of God as truth and have experienced its reality in their own lives need to do the teaching. The skillful, practical application of spiritual truths to everyday situations is the method we need to use. This formula brings proven results.

FAMILIARITY CAN BE UNHEALTHY

A few years ago the American Surgeon General voiced his disapproval at the promotion of *safe sex*. He pondered how many new venereal diseases the licensing of promiscuity under the terminology of *safe sex* would create. Rather than deal with immorality, the root of promiscuity, our country promoted *safe sex*, attempting to deal with its by-products.

In America five hundred thousand individuals have died as a result of AIDS and its effects. In one year alone there were sixteen million new cases of venereal disease reported. A recent study showed that one out of every six Christian couples is affected by an incurable sexually transmitted disease. On a global scale, the epidemic of AIDS has grown to apocalyptic proportions. In some areas of Africa whole villages are becoming extinct.

FAMILIARITY CAN DESTROY THE SECRET

There is a longing within almost everyone for close friendships–perhaps even one special friend with whom to share the deepest secrets. Many have their first confrontation with secrets as they start school and are challenged with making new friends. Most people will share some secret with those whom they hope to win as friends. If their confidence is betrayed, the one who shared the secret becomes emotionally scarred. Some vow never to share their secrets with anyone again. Most, however, end up following the same pattern of sharing a secret in another attempt to form a bond of trust. Without maturity and an understanding of trust and true friendship, similar situations will occur over and over again.

Sharing the secret is the vehicle that helps form the bond. If the secret is revealed, the hurt is deep. The more personal the secret, the deeper the bond–and with its revelation, the deeper the hurt. So begins a life of scars, hurts, and pain dealing with bonding.

Within the physical relationship, the *secret* encompasses sexual expression through visual perception, touching and sexual intercourse. One's body is a precious gift from God. The Bible refers to it as a temple of the Holy Spirit. The privacy of the individual's body, and its sexual organs, is a special secret to be shared only with a marriage partner.

We grieve for those teens who have not been taught that their secret is a sacred trust–who think nothing of having sex on the first date. We know the future pain they will endure. They will pay a big price emotionally, and perhaps physically also. Their secret has been destroyed. It has lost its significance. Once the secret has been shared, it is no longer a secret.

The secret plays an important role in the depth of the marital bond. The more first-time experiences that a married couple can experience together, the greater the depth of the bond. They will share a deeper degree of trust, excitement and security in their relationship.

In our years of marriage counseling and ministry, we have observed that nearly every troubled marriage has experienced fallout from previous emotional or sexual bonding experiences. This is as true in first marriages, where one or both partners have bonded in some way with previous dating partners, as it is in second or third marriages.

In our society, virginity and maintaining sexual purity until marriage is considered almost archaic. The couple who on their marriage night share their innermost physical secret, engaging in sexual intercourse for the very first time with each other, experiences the type of bond God designed and blesses. These two share their secret only with each other. They experience the ultimate expression of their own sexuality within the covenant of marriage, under the protection and favor of God.

FAMILIARITY CAN PRODUCE UNREALISTIC COMPARISONS AND COMPETITION

When a marriage experiences trying times, one or both partners often desire to dig into the closet and pull out skeletons from past experiences. It's bad enough when a couple begins to accuse each other of past sins, but it is far worse when one or both silently relive the past, fantasizing about former relationships. Past relationships should not be used as a comparison. The mind has a way of remembering things as much better than they actually were.

When life's present situation seems bad, one's mind can trick him into believing that almost anything–past or future–would be better than what he has. Situations from the past become points of comparison–usually very unrealistic comparisons! The devil lies about the past, and conveniently keeps old skeletons handy, stored neatly in memories, ready to be recalled for the express purpose of fostering more dissatisfaction with the present. The best thing that can be done with old skeletons is to bury them–once and for all.

Marriage, with its routine and realities, can seem less than exciting at times. The expression of sexual love within the marriage can become part of the routine. When this occurs, an individual who has had multiple premarital sexual or emotional relationships can easily relive past experiences with other partners. This will never be productive, and will only cause further division within the marriage.

Society proposes that a variety of experience will help one to recognize what he really wants in a marriage partner. The truth is, the more emotional or sexual bonds formed prior to marriage, the more temptation there will be to make comparison after marriage. This type of *variety* will produce a catalogue of experiences, faces and body parts, which the devil can bring to remembrance at any time, to cause comparison and division within future relationships. Apart from a supernatural healing of memories, those past premarital experiences will dramatically affect the relationship with a marriage partner.

FAMILIARITY CAN LESSEN SELF-CONTROL

"They were given over to a reprobate mind, and they turned the truth into a lie." Romans 1:28

Exposure to ungodly practices will produce sin, which in turn produces death. In Romans 6:23 it says, *"The wages of sin is death."* Most people do not understand that they walk on the path toward sin before they actually commit sin. That's where boundaries, limitations, principles and ethics come into play. They exist for protection.

An individual needs to set standards. He must make the decision to say, *"Here's where I draw the line. This is godly, but this is not."* Parents need to help their children set boundaries and limitations *before* they are needed. If you haven't established guidelines with your child prior to him finding himself in a situation requiring them, he will have no principles to protect himself in the moment of temptation.

Anyone who plays with fire stands the chance of getting burned. Experimenting with any form of physical familiarity can lead to deeper involvement–often deeper than wanted or expected. Parents must help their children establish standards based on biblical values, not on what feels good or what other teens, television or society embraces.

FAMILIARITY CAN PRODUCE A POOR SELF-IMAGE

When not done according to God's plan, bonding emotionally or physically can destroy self-worth. When someone becomes too familiar with sexual things outside of God's plan, whether as a participant or spectator, that individual comes under conviction. Conviction is a good thing. It is the Holy Spirit's safeguard to bring him to a point of repentance. If he does not repent and change his conduct, condemnation sets in. Condemnation brings guilt, which eventually produces shame and a sense of worthlessness. This usually engenders depression, which ironically begets more sinful involvement. Condemnation feeds its victim the lie, *"You're already doing it. You might as well do a little more. You've already blown it."*

This pattern of thinking is incorrect. Romans 8:1 instructs, *"There is therefore now no condemnation to them that are in Christ Jesus, who walk not after the flesh."*

A parent should help his child understand that when he is following God's plan and experiencing conviction, the Holy Spirit is trying to show him something. He must pay attention and make the necessary changes. If he is following God's plan and experiencing condemnation, it is an attack from the devil. The devil is a liar, and his condemnation is a lie–*if* God's plan is really being followed. Only the person knows if his heart is clean, if his motives are pure. The fruit evidenced by an individual's lifestyle, however, will prove this.

If one follows the passion of his flesh, he will first encounter conviction. If he does not repent and change, he will experience condemnation. He will have feelings of filthiness and unworthiness. He will develop a poor self-image. He will not like himself. If someone is having feelings such as these, he must examine himself. He should ask the question, *"Am I living as Christ would have me live?"*

The only way to eliminate condemnation is to make the decision to repent, turn away from sinfulness, and change one's mind and actions. God not only forgives. He forgives the past and *remembers it no more*. If one truly has changed his behavior, his repentance was real. God no longer remembers how someone was before. He sees him as the new creation he has become.

FAMILIARITY CAN DESTROY SPIRITUAL LIFE

The first commandment states quite clearly, *"Thou shalt have no other gods before Me."* Whenever anything is put above God's plan, it has become an idol. Ungodly sexual activity is a form of idolatry. Whenever someone steps outside of God's will, his fellowship with God is affected. When he becomes familiar with another person in an ungodly manner, separation from God takes place.

When one pleases himself and continues to sin rather than follow biblical principles, it's just like saying, *"God, what I want is more important than what you want."* That person has made a decision to allow his own desires to determine his behavior. He has chosen to set himself as more important than God's Word.

Following God's principles produces a blessing. To experience the blessing of God, one must follow His Word. In II Chronicles 15:2 it says, *"I am with you while you be with Me. If you seek Me, you will find Me."*

To experience God's direction, one must establish a relationship with Him and listen to His voice. If one wants to have the things he asks God for fulfilled, he needs to establish the kind of relationship with Him in which he is doing what He says.

John 15:7 instructs, *"If you abide in Me and My words abide in you, you shall ask what you will and it shall be given unto you."*

Sexual purity begins with simple things, like the way a teenager dresses. A parent should instruct his child in how to dress in a modest fashion. A teen's style of clothing can be very attractive, even vogue, without being revealing or in poor taste. He or she shouldn't be so willing to share his or her secret with others. Showing every bulge and curve may draw attention, but it won't be the type of attention that will be healthy–spiritually, emotionally or physically.

A teenager must be shown the value of, and the ways in which, he can guard his ears, eyes and hands from those willing to share his secrets. He must be shown the value of choosing friends who will respect him for his point of view–friends who will honor his principles. He needs to be taught the principles so that he can come up with his own ideas to keep his relationships pure by spending time with those who adhere to the same godly instruction he does. The goal is to help him understand he must not allow himself to get into situations where he might be tempted to compromise his values. Listening to godly authority and taking counsel from those who are truly concerned about his spiritual welfare is a by-product of a good relationship.

The Word of God says that although we are in the world, we are not to be a part of it. Teenagers need to use wisdom in every area of their lives, and parents need to help them in this process. Today there are both male and female qualified professionals. Whenever possible, it is usually best to secure services from a doctor or counselor of the same sex. This helps keep the secret and reduces the temptation for any misconduct. Titus 2:4 advises, *"Let the older women teach the younger women."* This is not only good scriptural advice, but it is also a safe practice to follow.

Robin was fifteen, a straight "A" student and a cheerleader. She had been her class homecoming representative two years in a row. Most of the boys in her school would have given anything to go out with her, but she had been going steady for two years with

David. David was on the football team and was also a good student. They both attended the same church and were together most of the time. Their parents were good friends, so it was very convenient for them to spend time together.

Their youth pastor was very concerned about their intimacy, and had on several occasions reprimanded them for PDA (public display of affection). The youth pastor had met with David and Robin, sharing his concern. He even met with both sets of parents. The parents actually reprimanded the youth pastor and told him to quit harassing their kids. They assured him that their children were intelligent young people who wouldn't do anything to jeopardize their bright futures.

Before Robin turned sixteen she became pregnant. Her parents were furious with her and David. Because of the families' convictions, they decided that Robin's mother would care for the baby while Robin finished school. David and Robin wanted to get married, but the parents would not let that happen. Both parents had dreams of their kids getting college degrees and then perhaps getting married.

The baby changed all of that. David and Robin's relationship was never the same. Before long his family moved and he made no attempt to contact Robin.

Chapter 4

HOW BONDING TAKES PLACE

The most practical explanation of the bonding process is found in the woodworking shop. When the carpenter wants to join two pieces of wood, he puts a dab of glue on each piece and then presses them together. He usually places a clamp on the joint and allows it to dry for some time. *Voila!* He has formed a bond between the two. The two pieces are no longer separate. It is just as if they have become one piece.

Properly glued, this new piece composed of the two glued pieces, will be stronger than the two were individually! In fact, if the carpenter begins with good, quality wood having smooth edges, and if the gluing is done properly, he will end up with an almost indestructible bond. The damage caused by attempting to separate the two pieces will usually ruin the wood. You could end up with a pile of splinters. Damage results when even the smallest amount of glue is applied to the two pieces and they are detached. The glue actually pulls a portion of the wood away from one piece, leaving it stuck to the other piece. The one piece has lost some of itself, while the other piece has extra parts stuck to it.

If you try to glue any two splintered pieces of wood together just the way they are, it will be very hard to facilitate any kind of lasting bond. Before a new bond can be achieved, any carpenter knows that he must go through a great deal of sanding, filing, shaving and planing to smooth the rough splintered edge into one that is clean, ready to bond again. It is obvious that a portion of the original piece will be lost in the process.

Whether we are dealing with spiritual, emotional, or physical bonding, the principle is basically the same.

Spiritually we bond with others through church or spiritually-related activities. If an offense arises between two Christians, and is left unresolved, it could result in a fragmentation, a separation of their spiritual bond. The hurt incurred may affect the success of future relationships with other fellow Christians. If the offense was incurred because of something within a church body, a separation from the church or a rift in one's relationship with God can result. The world is full of splintered Christians.

Before someone who has incurred a broken spiritual bond can be used in leadership–or even establish new bonds within the church–he must experience the sanding, planing and smoothing process of the Holy Spirit to bring healing.

Emotionally we all have, at one time or another, become bonded with someone who betrayed our trust. Emotional break-ups can sometimes affect us more adversely than any other type. Anger, unforgiveness and bitterness can be by-products of an emotional bond that has been broken. Experiencing emotional splintering may harden a person and cause him to be less open in another relationship. Even when forgiveness is applied, it still may take a lot of time to get over the hurt that was experienced.

Many couples begin their relationship as splintered individuals. They may be emotionally splintered as the result of a broken trust, or physically splintered because of sexual impurity. Usually they have come out of one relationship still reeling from the hurts of the first, never fully healed before attempting to develop a new relationship. Broken homes, broken friendships, multiple sexual partners, and broken promises have been the causes for the break in the bond, leaving wounded individuals like rough pieces of wood, with jagged edges, splinters and extra junk firmly attached to the surface.

Two splintered individuals, like the two splintered pieces of wood, will find difficulty in forming a solid bond between them. Two splintered individuals will find difficulty in establishing a trusting, loving marriage. Because of the broken bonds of the past, the chances of divorce become greater in each sequential marriage. Most individuals enter their next relationship still wounded by the hurts and problems of the last. Unless they receive counseling and get healed, these two splintered lives will form an unstable bond–which usually will not hold when pressure is applied.

PHYSICAL BONDING

Physical bonding usually follows natural steps of progression. Understanding this progression can help an individual to set guidelines and standards for physical involvement.

The first step in physical bonding is *eye-to-body*. What usually happens is when a person sees someone to whom he is attracted, his internal love-alert system goes off. If he is truly interested in getting to know more about that individual, step two commences.

The second step is *eye-to-eye*. At this point the individual attempts to make eye contact. The Word says that the eye is the window to the soul. The love alert system goes into the discerning mode as one individual peers into the eyes of the other. Rejection or acceptance is conveyed. If there is rejection, the process ends, and very little splintering has taken place. If there is acceptance, the individual proceeds in attempting to establish more contact.

The third step is *voice-to-voice*. A greeting is conveyed and conversation begins. The individual may have liked what he initially saw, but upon further investigation, does not like what he hears. In the voice-to-voice stage he discovers backgrounds, attitudes, convictions, likes, dislikes, etc. Based upon what happens in this stage, the relationship ends or deepens.

There can be emotional splintering even in the initial stage of bonding. If one individual would like to see the relationship develop and the other individual has no interest in the relationship, someone is going to be hurt–but usually not hurt too badly. Hopefully, this will be a learning experience that can help the individuals determine how to form godly relationships and develop kindness toward whomever they meet. If the two individuals both have a desire to pursue the relationship, they will proceed to the next step.

The couple will soon be involved in the fourth step, the stage we label *hand-to-hand*. This step adds the element of touch, which normally activates the senses.

The couple will then move into the more advanced forms of touching, including the fifth and sixth steps, **hand-to-shoulder** (hugging) and **hand-to-waist** (caressing).

The fourth, fifth and sixth steps are listed in the order of usual progression, but the logical order of these three steps may be switched around. For example, godly individuals who have established a brother-sister relationship may have greeted each other with an appropriate hug before they felt any development of the sensual relationship. The original intent of their hug was a form of greeting, establishing a spiritual and emotional bond. When they begin to form a physical bond, the hug will take on a new meaning as it is now based upon the added element of sensual touching.

Steps seven and eight, **hand-to-head** and *face-to-face*, usually take place within a close proximity of time, as the relationship moves into a new level of intimacy and arousal with kissing.

Excessive kissing and caressing lead to stage nine, **hand-to-body**, where petting begins. Heavy petting induces stage ten, **hand-to-genitals**, stage eleven, **mouth-to-body**, and finally stage twelve, **sexual intercourse**.

It is vital for a parent to instruct his child, when the information is age-appropriate, about the progression involved in these steps. The Christian parent needs to suggest guidelines concerning what is appropriate conduct at each stage. He needs to help his child set standards of where to draw the line.

Most Christians would agree that the final four steps are intended for marriage only. There are many Christians who are holding themselves accountable to a higher standard, feeling that anything beyond step six should not be entered into prior to marriage. In our travels we have met couples who have agreed not to kiss before marriage. An individual must determine if such a standard is desired and appropriate for himself.

Each step of the progression brings individuals into a deeper bond. As evaluation for the decision of setting limitations for courtship, we would mention once again that the most *firsts* a couple can enter into together, the stronger the bond they will develop. For a solid marriage relationship, one should consider how many firsts he will experience with *anyone* before he finds the *someone* God has for him. Prior to the wedding ceremony, when the covenant is established before God and witnesses, sexual intercourse is a sin.

The key to fulfillment in a physical relationship is following God's timetable and remaining sexually pure. Many young people today are taking a stand for sexual abstinence, but they are becoming involved in other forms of sexual play. They condone their conduct by maintaining their virginity. They might as well say, *"I'll do anything and everything except actually have intercourse."* They have missed the point. Sex out of marriage is a sin, but so are many sexual activities. Sexual familiarity is not healthy when experienced outside the marriage relationship.

Joshua was so excited about spring break. He was in his senior year and was looking forward to getting out of school. Some of his buddies were going south for spring break and were looking for a week of fun in the sun. Spring break was everything Josh thought it would be–girls, parties and good times. At times Josh felt guilty about what he was doing. He often wondered what his mom and dad would think. The problem was that he knew.

One night his buddies went to a strip club. He always wondered what it would be like to be in one. Josh had never seen a woman naked, except in movies and magazines. He found it exciting, but he knew how wrong it was. It seemed to be pulling him in to something that he knew was evil. As they left the club a couple of girls approached and talked to one of Josh's buddies. When he asked the buddy what that was all about, his buddy just laughed and said, "Oh you'll see."

Shortly after they got back to their motel there was a knock on the door. At the door were the girls they saw at the club. They entered the room and removed their clothes. They took turns having sex with Josh and his friends. Josh knew it was wrong, but he kept justifying his actions by telling himself it was just spring break and everyone was doing it. Josh went home with more than a real story to remember. His first sexual experience was with a hooker, and he received a STD.

Chapter 5

GODLY GUIDELINES

Children generally become inquisitive about sex and boy-girl relationships between the ages of ten and fourteen, depending upon their maturity level and peer group relationships. We believe that somewhere in that age level, a father and mother should be open with their child, sharing the blessings of God's plan and the consequences of not following it.

Teenagers need to be properly instructed before they become improperly experienced. We established a code of dating ethics with our own children. Not only did we establish the *thou shalt nots* but we explained the *why nots*. We talked frequently and openly with our children, using behavior-appropriate, age-appropriate instruction.

Rules and regulations without relationship breed rebellion within children. Many parents tell their children what not to do, but they don't explain why they shouldn't do it. Often parents will threaten their children with consequences for improper sexual behavior, but seldom will they explain what proper sexual behavior entails.

When forming a people set apart unto Himself, God established the Law. One day He met with Moses on a mountain and gave him the *Ten Commandments*. Genesis 20:2-17 gives this account: *"I am the Lord your God, who brought you out of the land of Egypt, out of the house of bondage. You shall have no other gods before Me . . . You shall not make for yourself a carved image . . . You shall not take the name of the Lord your God in vain . . . Remember the Sabbath day to keep it holy . . . Honor your father and mother . . . You shall not murder . . . You shall not commit adultery . . . You shall not steal . . . You shall not bear false witness against your neighbor . . . You shall not covet your neighbor's house . . . You shall not covet your neighbor's wife, nor his male servant, not his female servant, nor his ox, nor his donkey, nor anything that is your neighbor's."*

God gave the Law as a curb to keep us on the straight and narrow path, and as a mirror with which to look back upon our journey, learning from our failures and measuring our progress. The *Ten Commandments* are the foundation of all rules and regulations. The grace of God should motivate us to keep the Law out of love for Him.

The *Law of Diminishing Returns* teaches that whatever step you take, the tendency is always to proceed to the next step, not go backwards. In the physical relationship, that translates into: ***whatever behavior was exhibited in your last relationship, will be practiced in the next one, progressing further in the next than you did in the past***. An individual usually finds that he needs to experience more emotionally and physically in a new relationship to prove that it is better than the past one. Once experienced, it takes a real move of God to reverse patterns of sexual behavior.

Since Semantic people did not practice dating, there is nothing directly written about it in the Bible. Most marriages were arranged by the families. The couples rarely had any private time before the marriage. The relationship began at the marriage feast and developed through covenant commitment, not physical attraction. There are many within Christianity who feel that the marriage arranged by the parents is a still a good idea! Most teenagers shudder to think of whom their parents would choose for them.

We believe that if parents allow their children to date, the parents need to help their children set up standards. The dating stage needs to be a time of constant communication, when the parents pray for and with their children. Teenagers need to respect their parents, no matter how much they may disagree with their parents' ideas. By showing respect and being obedient, God can do a work in the child's heart as well as the hearts of the parents.

Together, parents need to contemplate the following questions, coming into unity on their response before their children ask. When the children ask, or when the time is appropriate, they can show agreement in addressing these issues with their children. Teens and young adults need to consider these questions before the occasion arises and they will need the answers.

- Will we allow our children to date?
- What age or maturity level will determine when our children will be allowed to date?
- What kinds of activities will be allowed?
- How frequently will we allow our children to go out?
- Will our children be allowed to date non-Christians?
- What standards and guidelines do we want to set for dating?
- What type of physical intimacy should be condoned, and when will it be allowed?

- What will we share with our children about our own dating experience?
- What counsel will we give our children regarding how open they should be in sharing things about themselves?
- What will we say to our children about date rape?
- What will be the consequences for our children's non-compliance with our rules regarding dating?
- What could go wrong on their dates?
- If our child finds himself in a difficult or compromising situation, what action should he take?

Ever since our children were little, we ministered to them that our priorities are God first and family second. Dating, jobs, friendships and other activities never interfered with that order.

We believe that parents should encourage their children to be deeply involved in church activities, and allow them great flexibility with group activities involving church kids–as long as they know the kids, their parents and their home lives.

When our children entered high school, we would allow our children to go to school activities, movies, skating, swimming, and out to eat after youth group with mixed groups–comprised of both boys and girls. They learned that the *group* requirement was not only a safe practice, but could be great fun. Usually the group not only included their peers, but their siblings as well, as our kids were very close in age–all three in high school at the same time.

Parents should explain to their children that talking in a group is easier, as there are lots of ideas to share. Whether the shy type or the leader type, being in a group of kids who share common godly principles can help develop maturity and self-identity.

For us, with all three of our children usually being in the same group, it also was easy for us to keep tabs on what was going on. We discouraged *one-on-one* dating until they became older teens. Even then we discouraged any type of exclusivity or going steady, until after high school. We allowed our children to have a *date* for special school events like Homecoming and Prom. Even for those events, we encouraged them to go in a group with several other couples who were also Christians and had similar dating standards. We also supervised to make sure it met *our* standards. Whenever possible, we were chaperones for the school or youth group events.

We stressed that for a child of God who wants to please Him, God will reveal the one who is to become their spouse. We acknowledged the scripture in Proverbs 18:22 where it says, *"He who finds a wife finds a good thing,"* but believed that finding that special person didn't need to be an all-out hunt, sampling one person after the other.

We did not allow our children to date a non-Christian. This was our personal conviction, based on the leading of the Holy Spirit and our understanding of Scripture. We understood about winning the lost, and we taught our children to be involved in evangelism. The personal conviction we portrayed to our kids was, *"Win the lost to Christ, but you can't date the lost. You can only date Christians."* Experience and years of observation have proven missionary dating can be dangerous.

Scripture is very explicit about being unequally yoked. II Corinthians 6:14 says, *"Be ye not unequally yoked together with unbelievers: for what fellowship hath righteousness with unrighteousness? And what communion hath light with darkness."*

Parents need to instruct their children about the differences in temperaments, upbringing, education, economics and spiritual training. Although these factors in themselves are not necessarily the determining elements in establishing a relationship, they do influence the relationship. Most parents learn these things through experience–just as we did. Part of parenting a teenager is sharing wisdom in these areas as counsel for your child.

A parent should know who his child is out with, whether as a group function or on a date. Certainly the responsible Christian parent should meet the young man or woman who will be spending time with his child prior to the date.

When a young man wanted to ask one of our daughters to go out on a date, our girls were instructed to tell him that he would have to call their father and ask his permission. Our girls found this to be a great protection device. Dad had the opportunity to find out about the boy, his family, his personal commitment to Christ, and his plans for the evening. If the guy's intentions were wrong, he usually wouldn't call, or survive the *interview*.

If a guy asked one of our girls to go out, but she didn't want to go, she shared that with Dad, and he became the one to say, *"No."* The girls found this to be a great way to deal with some guy who was hassling them or had wrong intentions–let Dad handle it!

We have always stressed that God's progression for physical bonding begins in the spiritual, where the relationship starts as brother and sister in Christ. It then moves into the emotional, involving the couple's desire to become friends. Actual physical bonding is a result of a healthy and mature development of the spiritual and emotional, with clear direction from the Lord to pursue deepening the relationship.

It is important to clarify the type of intimacy God allows. Every relationship begins with steps one, two and three. As we have studied Scripture and watched the bonding process at work, we are convinced that the physical (from steps four and onward) should not be entered into until a relationship has developed to the point where each sees the other as a *possible* marriage candidate. In other words, even though you might not be ready to get married at this point, this person meets the qualifications of one you *could* possibly marry some time–no matter how distant–in the future.

The teenager should be taught to consider questions like: *Does he or she possess the qualities and Christian values which I am looking for in a mate? Are the basics present? Does he or she believe the same way I do about sex and marriage? Has his home life produced fruit similar to mine? Are our ideals similar? Does he or she meet the standards I have set for myself?*

Depending upon the standards and boundaries which have been established, a seasoned relationship might enter into steps four through seven. Hand-holding, some hugging, and a kiss good night may be in order for the relationship which has developed into a more serious commitment. It should already be established that given time, maturity and further development, this relationship could end up in marriage. Remember, with each progressive step it becomes easier to move on and more difficult to back up.

Steps four through seven should be entered into responsibly. We advise a very limited, controlled, God-led progression. The engaged couple, wanting to do it God's way, should pray and seek God for the limitations to place on their relationship. Don't succumb to the lie, *"We're getting married so what does it matter anyhow."* Excessive petting and nudity are like playing Russian Roulette! Teens need to adopt a standard which helps them save the secret, use restraint and self-control and shows respect for each other. The honeymoon should be something special! Marriage should begin with the purity and innocence that God intended.

"For this cause a man shall leave his father and mother, and shall cleave to his wife; and the two shall become one flesh." Ephesians 5:31.

Marriage is sacred. God refers to it as a holy thing. The Catholic church includes holy matrimony on its list of sacraments. The development of a relationship which leads to marriage is a deeply spiritual experience. *Love American Style* is not God's style.   When bonding takes place according to God's guidelines and results in marriage, it truly will be the most spiritual experience a human being can have.

Rick moved to town in the fifth grade. Joleene had a crush on him from the day they met. She was very shy, and never quite had the nerve to approach him. She, however, was quite sure that he liked her. Every time they would pass in the hall he would smile and greet her. He never seemed interested in other girls and was involved in every sport, and very popular. Rick and Joleene were elected as the sophomore class prom representatives. Usually couples who were elected went to the prom dance together. For Joleene this was her dream come true. When Rick asked someone else to be his date, Joleene was crushed, and even missed a couple days of school.   The prom was an event to remember. But for Joleene's family, it is re-membered as the night Joleene took a gun and killed herself over a disappointing emotional bonding ex-perience.

Chapter 6

THE COVENANT OF MARRIAGE

Marriage is the single most important decision (besides salvation) that one will ever make. It is a once in a lifetime decision that will bring either a lifetime of love and fulfillment or heartache and pain.

Will you live together in the holy estate of matrimony? Will you love, comfort, honor and keep, for richer, for poorer, in sickness and in health; and forsaking all others, keep thee only unto yourselves, so long as you both shall live? If so, answer "I do."

What happened to the *"I do's"*? We live in a society of the *I won'ts, I can'ts,* and the *I don'ts.* We remember the day when a man's word was his pledge. When a person said *"I do"* or *"I will"* it didn't mean *I might, I could, maybe, who knows*! It meant it would definitely be accomplished, no question about it.

The *"I do"* of marriage is the biggest *"I do"* of them all. It means *whatever I do, I'll do with you forever.*

Forever is a *loooooonnnnnggg* time! It may mean fifty or sixty years, filled with many challenges and opportunities to wish you hadn't said *"I do."* More than the best man, maid of honor, and all the guests, God will hear the *"I do"* vowed at your marriage.

It is important to understand that marriage is a covenant. Marriage is the most sacred of all human covenants. If ever there is an *"I do"* that shouldn't be taken lightly, it is the marriage covenant. The family and the nation are paying a terrible price for the disregard of this most holy covenant. The breaking of the covenant sealed by those two little words, *"I do,"* has caused untold pain and heartache. That is not what God intended for marriage. He offers a better plan, a better way.

The Bible itself is divided into two groupings: the Old Covenant and the New Covenant. The Old Covenant or Old Testament is an account of God's working with the children of Israel and the covenants made with that group of people prior to the birth of Christ.

"But with thee will I establish my covenant; and thou shalt come into the ark, thou, and thy sons, and thy wife, and thy sons' wives with thee. And I will establish my covenant with you; neither shall all flesh be cut off any more by the waters of a flood; neither shall there any more be a flood to destroy the earth. This is

the token of the covenant which I make between me and you, and every living creature that is with you, for perpetual generations. I do set my bow in the cloud, and it shall be a token of a covenant between me and the earth." (Genesis 6:18, 11-13)

In the Genesis account we see God establish a covenant with Noah. Noah was spared from the destruction of the earth by the flood because of his commitment to God. Noah was a covenant man, a covenant maker and keeper. God's covenant with Noah established a promise that the earth would never again be destroyed by a flood. This provision was established as a generational covenant. As with most covenants made by God, there was a sign, some kind of symbol, act, or ritual, that stood as a reminder of the covenant made. In the case of Noah, it was the rainbow which continues today as a reminder of the covenant made.

"I will establish my covenant between me and thy seed after thee in their generation for an everlasting covenant, to be God unto thee and to thy seed after thee. This is my covenant, which you shall keep between me and you and thy seed after thee; every man child among you shall be circumcised . . . and it shall be a token of the covenant betwixt me and you." Genesis 17:7,10,11

In this example God established a covenant with Abraham and the entire nation of the children of Israel. God offered Abraham the promise of a good land and total provision for Abraham and his descendants. In this covenant there was a condition: the people must be committed and faithful to God, and they must carry out the rite of circumcision.

The letting of blood played a major role in the sealing of most of the covenants made in the Old Covenant. Blood was life; no blood, no life. All through the Old Testament we see the blood covenant as a reoccurring theme. When a covenant was made, it was usually sealed with an animal sacrifice. The letting of blood expressed the seriousness of the covenant. The one making the covenant would place his hands upon the head of the animal as an act of transfer. It made a statement that the covenant-maker would give his life to see that this covenant was carried out.

The frequent practice of sacrifice in the Old Testament was a constant reminder of the covenants made with God. Circumcision was the first time God required a *personal* letting of blood to seal the covenant. It was a permanent reminder to those who were circumcised of the covenant they made.

"Ye shall serve the Lord thy God, and He shall bless thy bread and thy water; and I will take sickness away

from the midst of thee. There shall nothing cast their young, nor be barren, in thy land; the number of thy days I will fulfill." Exodus 23:25,26

Most covenants were conditional. In this one, God expected His people to serve Him. Why wouldn't they want to? Service to God brings the blessings of provision, health, blessings for offspring and long life.

"Then Jonathan and David made a covenant, because he loved him as his own soul. And Jonathan stripped himself of the robe that was upon him, and gave it to David and his garments, even to his sword, and to his bow, and to his girdle." I Samuel 18:3,4

In the covenant made between Jonathan and David, an exchange of possessions took place. They exchanged their robes (which denoted their positions of authority and also were symbols of their wealth), their swords and bows (which were their protection), and their belts (an expression of making one's self vulnerable to the other). The bottom line was, *"What's mine is yours. I'll defend and protect you and your children."*

The New Covenant begins with the ultimate personal sacrifice–that of Christ laying down His life for mankind. The cross stands today as the symbol of sacrifice and the blood that was shed for our salvation.

"The Lord hath been witness between thee and the wife of thy youth, against whom thou hast dealt treacherously; yet is she thy companion; and the wife of thy covenant. And did not he make one? . . . That He might seek a godly seed." Malachi 2:14,15

Marriage is a covenant. It is the most sacred of covenants. To cause the insight from the scriptures and examples we've explored to become effective in our lives, we must learn from them. We must choose to obey God's Word rather than be led by our own emotions, desires or the accepted practices of the world.

The covenant of marriage is for a lifetime. Christ taught that we would not be given in marriage in heaven. One's commitment is to be for as long as he is alive on earth. God's perfect intention and plan for man was that there would be no divorce. Jesus said that *for the hardness of the hearts* divorce was allowed. In divorce, quite commonly one spouse chooses not to forgive. This isn't always the case, but it is more often than not. God commands us to forgive one another so that we can be forgiven by Him. Even in the case of adultery, the highest good would be to forgive and work through the issues. God's grace is vast enough to cover shortcomings and heal hurts. He is able to give strength to "run the race."

The covenant of marriage is generational. Nothing has had a greater effect on the destruction of society over the last few decades than divorce. Divorce has single handedly set a course of destruction in family after family. The children usually suffer greatest, with more long-lasting effects than the parents. Divorce can set in motion a generational curse which can be broken only by the redemptive power of the Lord Jesus. In contrast, a couple who remains faithful to their covenant vow can set in motion generational blessings.

The covenant of marriage is a surrendering of rights. The "I do" should mean "I give you all of me. I give you my body, my money, my possessions, my dreams; I will protect you even if it costs me my life. I will open myself to you and make myself vulnerable in all truth. And I will practice forgiveness."

The covenant of marriage is under the blood. The woman is the only female in the animal kingdom that has a hymen. If a woman remains a virgin till marriage, unless some trauma has torn the hymen, there usually will be some sign of blood upon consummating the relationship with her husband. Even in His creation of the female, God was thorough.

Intercourse is for marriage only. The first act of sexual intercourse between the newly married husband and wife helps seal this most precious covenant. After the emotional commitment of the heart comes the verbal commitment–then the physical sealing of becoming one through a sexual relationship. Keep in mind that marriage is precious to God and is covered by Jesus' blood. If one has lost his virginity by moving outside of God's plan, he needs only confess it to God and accept His forgiveness. God is a restorer. He can restore purity, innocence and sanctity.

Duke loved girls. As a teenager, his quest was to see how many girls he could have sex with. When he was in his early twenties, he wanted to settle down and get married. He didn't want a relationship with the type of girls that he was accustomed to going out with. He wanted someone who was pure and wholesome. He wanted a girl who would be faithful and true–one he didn't have to be concerned with whom she had been with.

Miraculously, he found such a girl. She was willing to forgive his past and trust that he was a changed man. Their marriage seemed fine, but for Duke there was a continual struggle to be faithful. At first it was only an occasional glance at a pretty girl. Before long he was actively involved in pornography. When his wife found a credit card statement itemizing charges to porn sites, she was devastated. The fidelity and trust factor was broken. Even though he did not have a physical affair, they both were reminded of Jesus' own words, "He who looks on a woman to lust after her has already committed adultery with her in his heart."

Their relationship never was the same. Duke and his wife went through a lot of counseling, but she found it hard to reestablish the trust factor.

Chapter 7

MAKING THE CHOICE

Joshua was faced with leading people who didn't want to serve God. He stood before them one day and declared, *"As for me and my house, we will serve the Lord."* Joshua 24:15

Elijah stood before the children of Israel and said, *"How long will you falter between two opinions? If the Lord is God, follow Him; but if Baal, follow him."* I Kings 18:21

A decision needs to be made once and for all whether you are going to follow God's way or the world's way. There are only two teams in the game of life. The choice is between joining the *Kingdom All Stars* or the *Hell's Bells*. Romans 8:6 tells us, *"The mind set on the flesh leads to death and the mind set on the spirit leads to life."*

The choice is obvious, but with the pressures today, it takes real conviction to do it God's way. One must set a standard and stick to it–no matter what the cost. It is worth whatever price must be paid. It may mean discontinuing dating someone with whom a close relationship has developed. It might involve changing friends. If they cause a compromise of standards, find new friends. A teenager must understand that his body belongs to himself. God holds him responsible for his actions. *"But I was pressured,"* is not an excuse with God. Your child must determine that poor choices can ruin his self-image as well as his future. He must learn to say, *"No!"*

In Galatians 5:19-21 there is a list of the deeds of the flesh: *"Now the works of the flesh are evident, which are: adultery, fornication, uncleanness, licentiousness, idolatry, sorcery, hatred, contentions, jealousies, outbursts of wrath, selfish ambitions, dissensions, heresies, envy, murders, drunkenness, revelries, and the like; of which I tell you beforehand, just as I also told you in time past, that those who practice such things will not inherit the kingdom of God."*

The list begins with *"adultery, fornication, uncleanness . . . "* It ends with *". . . those who practice such things shall not inherit the kingdom of God."* This scripture is very specific about describing sins that are destructive. God has set up guidelines for our sexuality because He knows what will benefit us and produce an abundant life. God did not intend to keep us from having fun. He wants His children to have healthy, productive, joy-filled lives. He desires marriage to be an awesome relationship–filled with love, peace, intimacy and friendship.

In the Old Testament, the temple was the place where the presence of God resided. The priests sacrificed burnt offerings day and night to cover sin and establish the temple as a holy place.

Your child needs to understand that as a New Testament child of God, he has been chosen as the place in which God's Spirit and presence dwells. I Corinthians 3:16 states: *"Do you not know that you are the temple of God and that the Spirit of God dwells in you?"* The believer's body is the temple where God's Spirit abides. The sacrifice your child needs to make on a daily basis is that of holy living–maintaining a pure, God-pleasing lifestyle.

Christ prayed on the night of His betrayal, *"Father, make them one as we are one."* The human mind cannot begin to comprehend the depth of relationship between the Trinity. They are three, yet one. Co-equal, coeternal, yet separate. They flow in perfect harmony with one another–such perfect harmony that they are one. There is never any opposition or disagreement. They are separate in nature, yet single in purpose.

God is looking for that kind of oneness within the Church. He also wants that kind of oneness within marriage. *"The two shall become one."* No longer are there two individuals piloting separate courses, but two individuals piloting a course as one. They are one in purpose, one in flesh and one in spirit.

In the Christian marriage, God promises to bond with the man and the woman–blessing, directing and guarding their union. God's intent is for marriage to be the most fulfilling experience of human life. It starts with dating and the relationships built before marriage. Above all, it starts with commitment to Jesus Christ. As a parent, you must help your child to understand that he cannot allow his hormones to dictate and direct his life. He must be taught by example to let the Holy Spirit be his guide. He must be shown that doing it God's way is the best way.

THE GOD OF SECOND CHANCES

Many teens who hear this message might think, *"It's too late for me. I'm like the board that is all splintered. I've already messed up my life."* A parent needs to assure such a child that God wants to restore things for him.

I John 1:9 says, *"If we confess our sins, He is faithful and righteous to forgive us our sins and to cleanse us from all unrighteousness."*

Psalm 103:1-4 says, *"Bless the Lord, O my soul; and all that is within me, bless His holy name! Bless the Lord, O my soul, and forget not all His benefits: who forgives all our iniquities, who heals all our diseases, who redeems our life from destruction, who crowns us with loving kindness and tender mercies."*

Our God makes a way when things seem hopeless. All He requires of the one who sinned is that he confess his faults, turn from his sin and receive God's forgiveness and restoration. If your child has sinned in any area of his life, but especially in the area of sexual relationships, his restoration depends upon him repenting and turning away from the sinful behavior. He must tell God that he is sorry for his past sin, ask for His forgiveness, and ask for His help to lead a pure sexual lifestyle. He must ask God to restore him so that he can enjoy the blessings of a godly relationship.

Physically, one cannot have his virginity restored. But emotionally, God can restore his self-image. And spiritually, God can restore a relationship with Him. One can't change the fact that he did sin–but God will forgive that sin. The past sin may be remembered by the one who sinned–but God forgets it. There is always a price paid for past sin–but God heals the scars. Psalm 103:12 says, *"As far as the east is from the west, so far has He removed our transgressions from us."* You can help your child receive healing for his mind from the memories and the guilt of the past.

You must teach him that he cannot allow condemnation to hinder him from going forward. Romans 8:1 shows us that, *"There is therefore now no condemnation to those who are in Christ Jesus, who do not walk according to the flesh, but according to the Spirit."*

He can start fresh. There is a new life ahead for him when he commits to doing it God's special way from here on. He can start over. It will give him a brand-new life and a bright, rewarding future. *"Therefore, if anyone is in Christ, he is a new creation; old things have passed away; behold, all things have become new."* II Corinthians 5:17

COMMIT TO VIRGINITY

We taught these principles to our children when they were young teenagers. We held a ceremony in our church in which many of our teenagers vowed to remain sexually pure, saving themselves for the person who would become their marriage partner. Many churches are now conducting *For Marriage Only* ceremonies, where parents present their children with a ring, locket or some reminder of the commitment to purity that they have made. In the ceremonies we conduct, we also presented the person making the commitment with a certificate commemorating that vow of purity. We encourage the parents to sign the certificate as witnesses of the commitment their child has made.

In the wedding ceremonies in our church, we made reference to the commitment to purity which was made as teenagers. During the ceremony the father removed the virginity ring from his daughter's hand, placing it into her husband's hand. We explained to the wedding guests that the ring had been given to her as the symbol of her vow to sexual purity. We instructed the groom that he was now the protector of the purity of their relationship. We feel this can be a very meaningful part of the wedding ceremony, and emphasizes the sanctity of two pure lives joined into one in holy matrimony.

Many young people have found following God's principles for sexual purity to be very rewarding. Because of taking a stand as teenagers, many married couples are reaping the benefits of a fulfilled married life.

As teenagers, Jill and Sam made decisions to live for Christ. They took vows of abstinence from sexual impurity till marriage. In their daily prayer times they asked the Lord to bring them their life partners.

Jill and Sam met at college. God revealed to both of them that their relationship was His choice. They dated, but also established strict guidelines to insure that they would not fall into temptation. They knew that during their courtship their spiritual and emotional bond was of the most importance.

The rest is history. They have now been married seven years and have three children. They have enjoyed, and plan to continue enjoying, the blessings of bonding God's way.

Restoring Integrity
to
Marriage
and the Family

Scott ♥ Cheri Scheer
and
Family Ministries

are dedicated to promoting family values and presenting practical teaching on marriage, parenting and family in Bible colleges, church services and through seminars, retreats and conferences.

Scott ♥ *Cheri Scheer*

ROCK YOUR WORLD MINISTRIES

James Scheer is one of the most dynamic youth speakers today. He travels throughout the United States and overseas, speaking in churches and at conferences, to young people and adults. Sharing his inspirational testimony, he challenges this generation of young men and women to *"Rock Their World"* for Jesus. His message to parents and adults is powerful.

James is dedicated to *raising up a righteous generation*, teaching young people to take a stand for honor, integrity and the kingdom of God, and challenging parents and adults to become mentors of the generation they lead.

For information on scheduling James Scheer as a speaker for your church or conference contact:

rockemail@excite.com

or the Family Ministries office at
1-800-749-9839

James Scheer

More Books

by Scott ♥ Cheri Scheer

Marriage Building Blocks – practical principles for building your marriage to last a lifetime.

"I Do" – practical insight for understanding the true significance of covenant and meaning of the wedding vows.

Raising Kids Right! – a Christian family approach to raising children with loving discipline. Tried and true methods to help you understand your child's needs and motivations. Practical, biblical advice to help you train your child to become obedient and lovable.

When a Child Goes to Heaven – the moving, true story of one family's tragedy. This book will bring comfort and closure to the "why" and grief resulting from the loss of a child.

Building a Strong Family Tree – Practical insight into the key ingredients all successful families have in common. Learn how to establish a legacy and promote a relationship with your children through which they will grow to love and respect you.